A PROCESSiON OF FLOWErS

By Becky Bereman Grimes

ISBN 1460942248
ISBN 978-1460942246

Published by Alternatives Unlimited
324 S. Brooks St.
Sheridan, WY 82801

Also by Becky Bereman Grimes

Leaf Art (Lefart):
A Joyful and Playful Look at Leaves...and some poems

Leaf Art ABC...and some dances

Destination: Mammoth Hot Springs for a Very Special
Event

Destination: Grand Canyon of the Yellowstone

A Procession of Flowers
(in 6 x 9 or 8 x 10)

From Flowers to Foliage

Bird Tails

Giddy-Up!
An original 2010 Leaf Art (lefart) creation by
Becky Bereman Grimes
au@vcn.com

'Procession of Flowers' and its sequel 'From Flowers to Foliage' came from our weekly fishing trips in the Big Horn Mountains from May to October in 2010.

I hope to give you a glimpse into the transitions the high mountain prairie made from week to week of that year.

This book is dedicated to the man I have loved for a lifetime, 'my' Charlie. "You are my sunshine, my only sunshine, I love the sun shine in your eyes and smile."

In the year 2010 on May 6th in the Wyoming town where we live there was 3 feet of snow when we went to check on the Canadian Goose on her nest. When we arrived at our fishing hole in the Big Horn Mountains on May 15th we were met by a wall of snow. It was a first for him! We were turned back again for two more weeks as well.

First Fish
June 2, 2010

Doing the trout boogie!

It wasn't until June 2nd that we were able to get to the stream. He was all business but I dilly dallied taking pictures. The beautiful Pasque flower, also known as Wild Crocus, Lion's Beard, Prairie Anemone, Blue Tulip or American Pustallia was the first flower.

There wasn't much else for me to photograph but the willows, so we fished.

Ride the River
June 9, 2010

Running full!

The Pasque Flowers bowed their heads in prayer as far as we could see. Up close they seemed to smile! Even the willow patch had changed color.

Forget-me-nots are a hard flower to photograph because they are so small. Zooming in will get everything around them but the flower is often blurred.

Fog Fishing
June 16, 2010

We Came, We Fished, We're Cold.

We saw more green on this trip.
Tucked into crevices were baby bluebells
and three perky shooting stars that
looked ready to blast off.

We spied the American Globeflower and a
White Shooting Star.

The lichens on the rock echoed the
color of the sage and willows.

A cowboy lost his pony
and these unadorned
aspens were backlit by fog.

My fishing rod posed in the fog.

Bigs' Fishing Trip
June 29, 2010

Bigs found the only porcupine we have
seen up here. The quills didn't seem to
damage her chin.

Fluorescent green lichen in the shape of Bigs. How perfect to see the Common Dog Violet today. It is called that due to its lack of perfume meaning it was "only suitable for dogs."

There is a fairy assigned to Violets which Cicely Mark Barker has beautifully illustrated.

What child does not love bluebells?

A Fine Day of Fishing
June 26,2010

Never come between a man and his fish.

There are some striking differences today. Sky dragons march across the sky, and it is an Irish green landscape dotted with buttercups. The willows were flowering and the dandelions were the largest I'd ever seen! Maybe everything just looks bigger and better on the mountain. The Sticky Cranesbill showed a bright face. We wondered, "Who is this color whirl of ruby red?"

Mountain Serviceberry climbed a stone and
Nuttails Larkspur was tucked between
granite. Everywhere we looked there were
Alpine Shooting Stars with dew on them.

The aspens
looked like they
were playing
Hokey Pokey,
putting their
backside in!

A fresh new
fawn got up,
looked around
and bawled
for its mom.

It saw me and
began to come
over. I told it
no, but loved
the chance to
see it so closely.

Over and Back
July 5th, 2010

He makes me laugh!

After the 4th of July in Cody, WY we stopped to see what had happened on the mountain since the prior week. We began our journey, as we had so many others, by hiking up this meadow.

As we crested the hill we saw that the late snow in May and the soaking rains in June had had an unprecedented effect on the floral landscape. There were wildflowers as far as the eye could see.

This bee found a sweet spot! There are several low larkspur found in Wyoming. Plants from this genus can be fatally poisonous to both human and animals.

Then we began
to walk toward
the stream and
we found
these jewels...

a bi-color lupine,
near a graduated
color bar lupine,
near the
lightest lupine...

there were
lupine
everywhere!

Sticky Cranesbill, also called Sticky Geranium, is one of several western Geraniums with pinkish-purple flowers. Richardson's Cranesbill has a white flower. Geranium comes from an ancient Greek word 'geranos' meaning
crane. It refers to the flower's 'beak.'

The ancient word referred to two kinds of chain dance. First, a dance invented, according to legend, by Theseus, who danced it for the first time in Delos after the rescue of seven youths and seven maidens from the Labyrinth. The intricate movements of the dance were supposed to represent being led out of the Labyrinth.

It also referred to a dance imitating the communication and mating of cranes.

Prairie Smoke, also known as Old Man's Whiskers or Purple Aven, is one of my favorite flowers to view through its fertilization process.

Forget-me-nots, Common Buttercup, Prairie Smoke, Western Bistort, Dandelion and Showy Locoweed, can you name more?

These white drifts of phlox scented the mountain so fragrantly that we wanted to invent an odor recorder!

This pair of coral paintbrush heralded the coming of the paintbrush!

Pale Indian Paintbrush is usually found in most of Alaska except S.E. Alaska but we found it here this summer.

There was a feeling of abundance as we approached the aspen grove. A red squirrel was prepared to protect it's cache. Its chatter and look warned, "Don't make one wrong move."

Flower Fishing
July 10, 2010

He does his imitation of a black crowned night heron.

Here are the proverbial cows in the meadow. This one looked like she was wearing a black hat. The bull wondered where his cows had gone. His bellows echoed through the hills.

I thought, "What a lucky mountain cow and calf to be able to spend the summer here!"

Remember the meadow slope last week? It sure doesn't look the same! The rock sentinel thinks something has changed too!

As we top the hill Charlie asked me how many different kinds of flowers we had seen.
I said, "Begin the count!" He kept track. I got to 60 by the time we had reached the stream to fish and it was only July! I also added ones from our daily walks along the paths by the ponds in town:

Prairie Crocus, Mountain Bluebells, White Shooting Star, Alpine Shooting Star, American Globeflower, Dog Violets, Blue-Pod Lupine, American Bistort, Arrow Leaf Balsam Root, Prairie Smoke, Dandelion, Rocky Mt. Phlox, Western Serviceberry, Nuttall's Larkspur, Subalpine Larkspur, Richardson's Cranesbill, Wild Iris, Golden Aster, Alpine Buttercup, Showy Locoweed, Sticky Cranesbill, Forget-me-nots, Desert Paintbrush, Giant Scarlet Paintbrush, Pale Indian Paintbrush, Tansy Leaf, Evening Primrose, Mariposa Daisy, Coulter's Globemallow, Yarrow, Blue Columbine, Prairie Flax, Fireweed, Wild Rose, Lanceleaf Coreopsis, Chickweed, Fendler's Waterleaf, Pussy Paws, White & Red Clover, Pearly Everlasting, Monument Plant...the list went on.

Last week's spectacularly unusual display of Blue Pod
Lupine was topped by a perfect specimen today. The
Rocky Mt. Phlox on a rock was a breathtakingly fragrant
sample of that species. The color of the Sticky Geranium
(Cranesbill) was beginning to make quite a show.

At the stream the
bluebells had grown
nearly three feet tall
and in many places
were hanging over
the water.

We walked from the ancient skeleton of a great tree to the youngster who has replaced it to start our fishing. Along the way we saw more samples of an unusually verdant Wyoming landscape. It was a challenge to identify them all. Can you?

Rodeo Days
Fishing
July 17, 2010

A Man and His Tree

Potentilla and buttercups accented the unusual Wyomng
Irish green. Prairie Smoke went to seed like a child's
pinwheel! These cabin bluebells had the advantage of
rainwater running off the roof. Pink granite complimented
the Bull Elephant Head flower. A lupine graced the fencepost.
Tucked into the grass Pussy Paws and phlox make 'Phlox and
polka dots.' We were overwhelmed by what we saw.

It was a riot of color! The forget-me-nots
were over a foot tall. Even the forest floor
was in bloom!

Remember the Sticky Cranesbill we saw in June and
early July? With the slow steady rain it had grown!

Tall coral paintbrush in the
willows surprised us as we
wound our way along the
stream bank. The elephant herd
was at the water for a drink.

Simply
beautiful
wherever
we
looked!

A study in fishing and
certainly a fisher
person's dream!

We followed the rainbows all the way home.

Looking west the sunset was apricot. We had seen an apricot paintbrush today.

To the east it was lavender. We would see a lavender paintbrush next week

Bright Blue
Fishing
July 24, 2010

Knee deep in foliage under a
bright blue sky. Let's fish!

On today's menu is a rather psychedelic Indian Paintbrush and these coral beauties. Oh, Oh, Oh the flowers were so beautiful!

The elephant head flowers would be gone by the next week so I loved having the herd as fishing buddies today. There were more elephants in the tall grass.

On our way down to the stream
we spotted this coyote pup. We
watched him trot down to warn
another pup who took off. Then he
laid down facing us. When we
broke
out of the rocks where we had
hidden he took off and was gone!

The rocks and willows
have ample space in
which to hide. A pair
of pups and a pair of
true blue lupine.

A Hallowed Day of Fishing
July 31, 2010

It was a really big fish!

Near where we saw the pups last week we saw
this very interesting piece of coyote art . Harebells
marched with Yarrow across the prairie and Prairie
Smoke seed was lifted by ancient sage arms.
The paintbrush were thick in the willows. We saw
at least 4 shades of lipstick colors including a
cheery pink blush and a quiet red.

August Breeze
August 7, 2010

You gave me shelter from the storm
in the lee of your mountainside.

There was a softness to that day.
Wild carrot along with yarrow and
cranesbill going to seed. Grasses
were beginning to dry out. We
welcomed two newcomers...the deep
purple buds of an Explorer Gentian and
the soft lavender of a Tahoka Daisy.
A harebell parade, some grass and a
rock, a pair of soft pink paintbrush and
beautiful harebell in sagebrush with
Western Serviceberry all
made their appearance.

A dazzling fluorescent pink Indian Paintbrush
in sage and a breathtaking storm over Twin Buttes!

Yum!!! Wild strawberries! When we had eaten our fill of the
delicious morsels I turned around and there was an Indian
Paintbrush the same size and color of the strawberries. We
went home with strawberry juice on our knees and elbows.

Breath of Fall
August 15, 2010

We went back the next
weekend for more luscious fruit.

Soft sagebrush in bloom, the cheerful daisy and the lush prairie blossoms of yarrow, wild onion, wild carrot and potentilla were once again as far as the eye could see!

A bright Tahoka Daisy said 'hello' with a smile. It was the largest we saw of that species.

When I began to search for the name of this new and lovely flower I read that the Explorer Gentian had been touted as the most beautiful of wildflowers. Beautiful indeed!

These soft pink paintbrush reminded me of pale ballerinas taking center stage for their solos.

The Smell of Rain
August 22, 2010

Just a small obstacle!

Cranesbill leaves changed to fall color amidst Harebell, Tahoka Daisies, Yarrow and thousands of stems from spent dandelions. A daisy duo shyly invited us to share a moment. Their center color was the shade of the passing cranesbill.

A storm came up quickly and we could see the rain moving towards us. Then it passed and a sunbeam landed at the head of where we were fishing. The sunbeam lit up the willows when it moved.

A bright cranesbill leaf made an appearance as we were leaving. The Sandhill cranes were in the hay meadows on our way home.

Bright Two
August 28, 2010

I marvel at the color these bright two share. How can two different species present themselves so?

A sudden storm came up on all sides; so we took cover in the willows. Once again we saw the rain marching down the stream. I did not notice until I uploaded my photos from the day that it had gotten so dark it turned the photos to grayscale. Then the light and the color gradually returned.

We saw a single stem of fireweed, some
strawberry and raspberry leaves and this
Monument Plant.

Then we followed rainbows home.

I hope you enjoyed this Procession of Flowers. There is a sequel to this story as we transition From Flowers to Foliage. Here is just a taste. This tree nearly sizzles!

www.ingramcontent.com/pod-product-compliance
Lightning Source LLC
Chambersburg PA
CBHW050829290526
45792CB00001B/317